· Let's Draw ·
CARTOON CHARACTERS

Dave Garbot

This library edition published in 2023 by Walter Foster Jr.,
an imprint of The Quarto Group
100 Cummings Center, Suite 265D
Beverly, MA 01915, USA.

© 2023 Quarto Publishing Group USA Inc.
Artwork © 2014, 2015, 2016 Dave Garbot
Illustrated and written by Dave Garbot

Distributed in the United States and Canada by
Lerner Publisher Services
241 First Avenue North
Minneapolis, MN 55401 U.S.A.
www.lernerbooks.com

First Library Edition

Library of Congress Cataloging-in-Publication Data

Names: Garbot, Dave, author.
Title: Let's draw cartoon characters / Dave Garbot.
Description: First library edition. | Beverly, MA : Walter Foster Jr.,
   2023. | Audience: Ages 8+ | Audience: Grades 4-6
Identifiers: LCCN 2022019947 | ISBN 9780760380895 (library binding)
Subjects: LCSH: Cartoon characters. | Drawing--Technique.
Classification: LCC NC1764 .G375 2023 | DDC 741.5/1--dc23/eng/20220707
LC record available at https://lccn.loc.gov/2022019947

Printed in USA
10 9 8 7 6 5 4 3 2

TABLE OF CONTENTS

CHAPTER ONE

AN INTRODUCTION TO CARTOONING

Welcome! Drawing cartoon characters is a lot of fun. There is no right or wrong way to draw them. It's all up to you and your imagination! Even if this is your first time drawing, this will be a lot of fun and something you can do over and over again. When you draw these silly, zany cartoon characters, it's important to relax and have fun. Don't worry about how nice your drawing looks or whether your lines are perfectly straight. Follow the steps and your cartoons will appear right before your very eyes! So get ready, grab your pencil and paper, and let's start drawing!

TOOLS AND MATERIALS

FACES AND FEATURES

There are so many ways to mix and match your favorite parts to create your own silly creations. Try some of these faces and features on your cartoon characters.

Eyes

Noses and Beaks

Ears

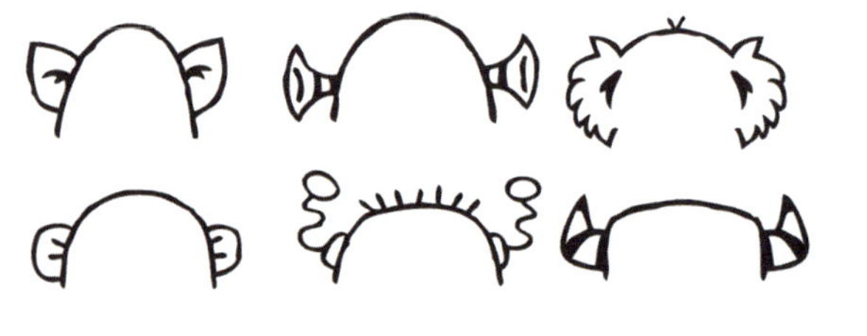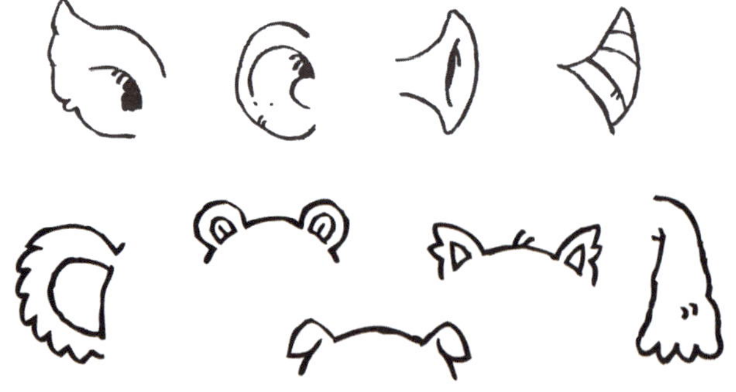

Mouths

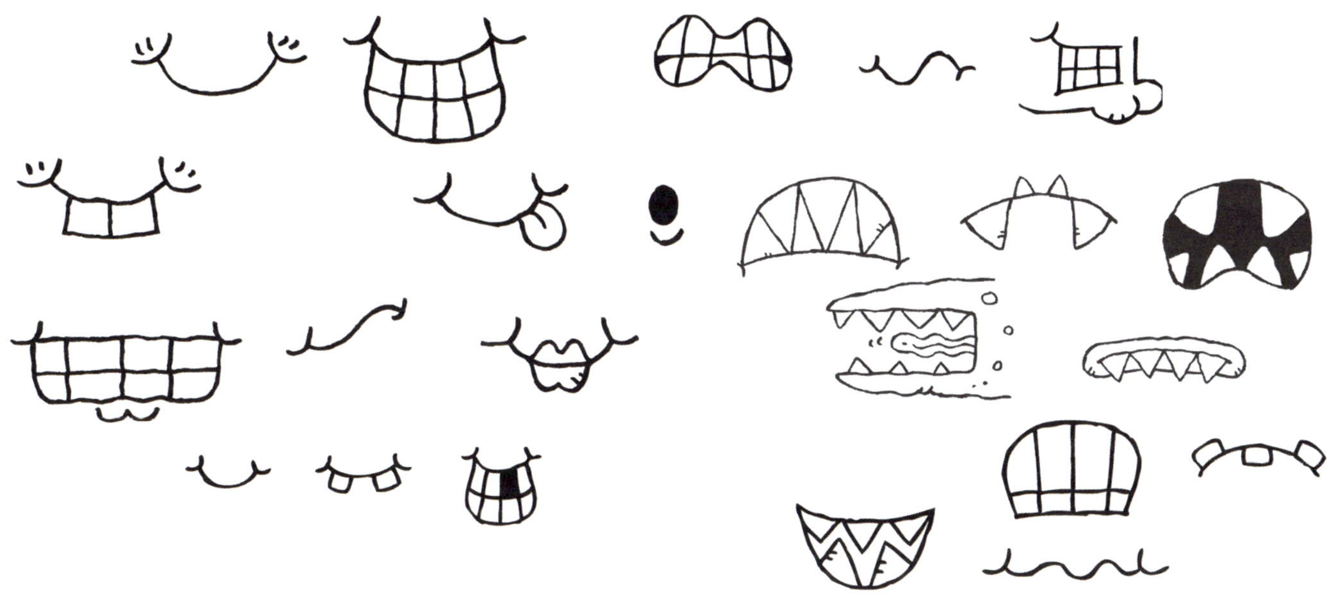

Feet

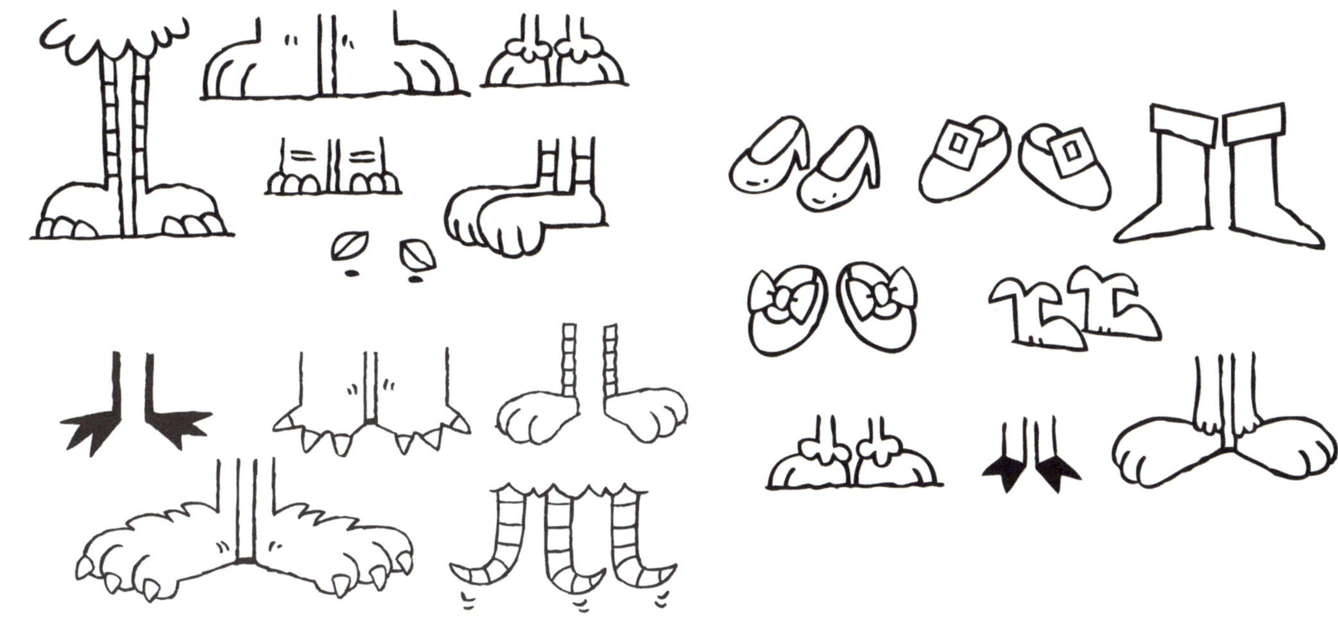

Tails

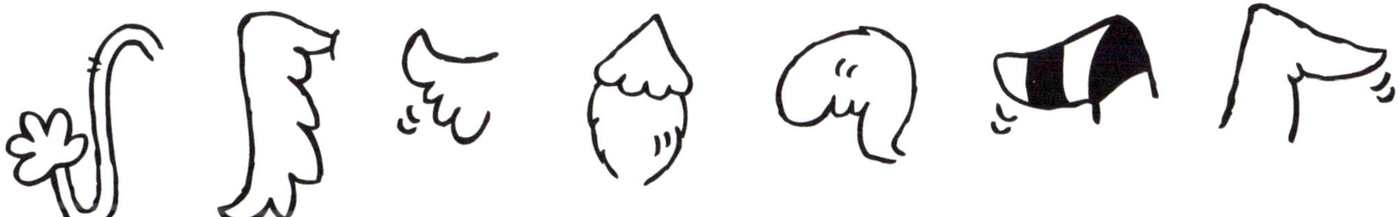

EXPRESSIONS

Expressions can tell a lot about our characters and how they feel. They are usually pretty happy, but maybe the character you draw is tired, surprised, or extra excited! You can use facial expressions and gestures to help express emotions and personality.

Happy

Sick

Confused

Worried

Amused

Surprised
Excited
Tired
Angry
Embarrassed
Content
Sad
Curious

ACCESSORIES

Sometimes characters like to dress up or carry funny objects with them.
Here are some ideas for snazzy accessories you can use.

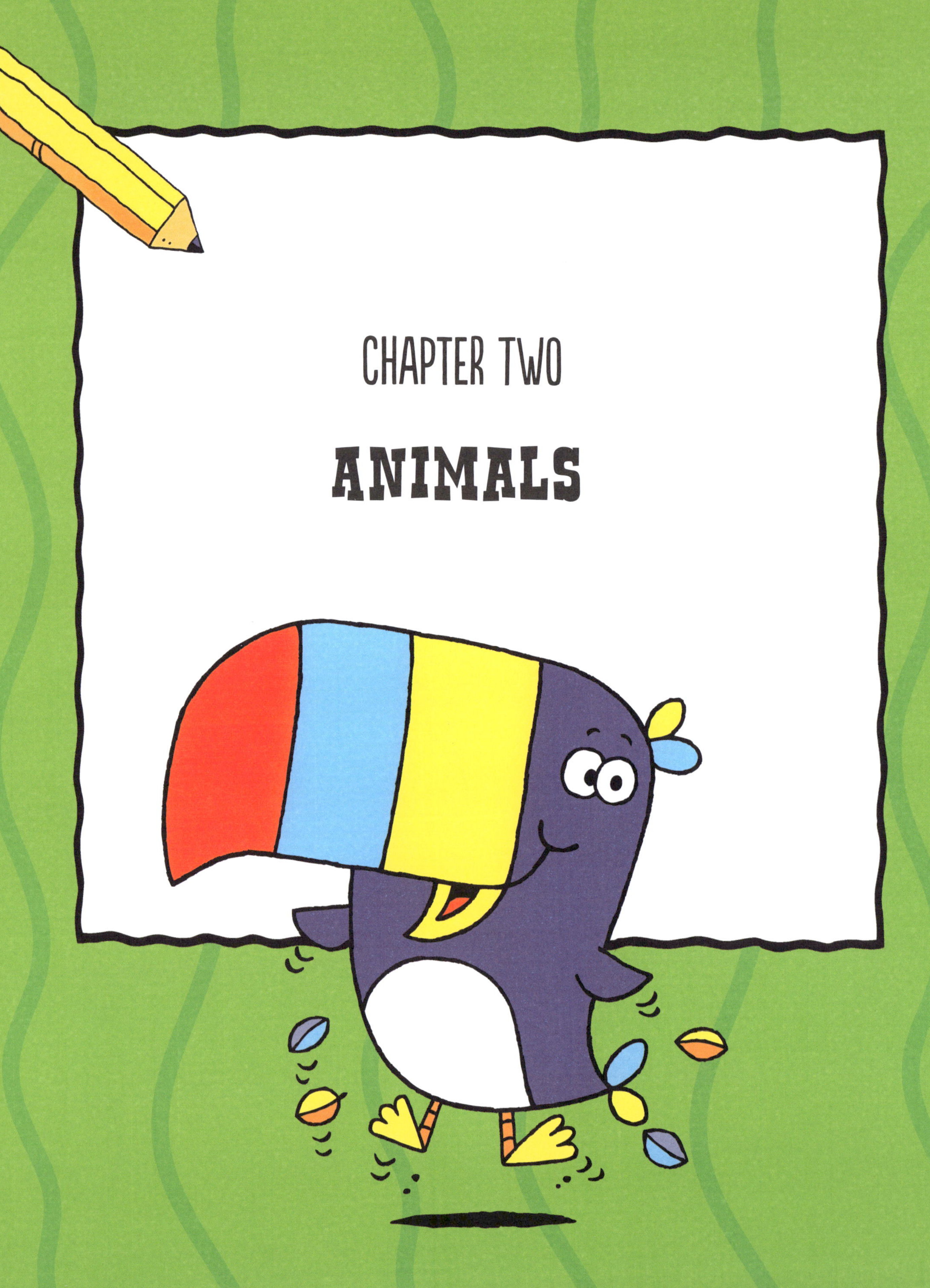

CHAPTER TWO

ANIMALS

BUNNY

This bunny has closed eyes, but can you draw them open? Hint: Try making your rectangle a little wider at the top in step 1.

TOUCAN

This is one happy toucan. Can you make a second bird that is much smaller?
Just follow the same steps!

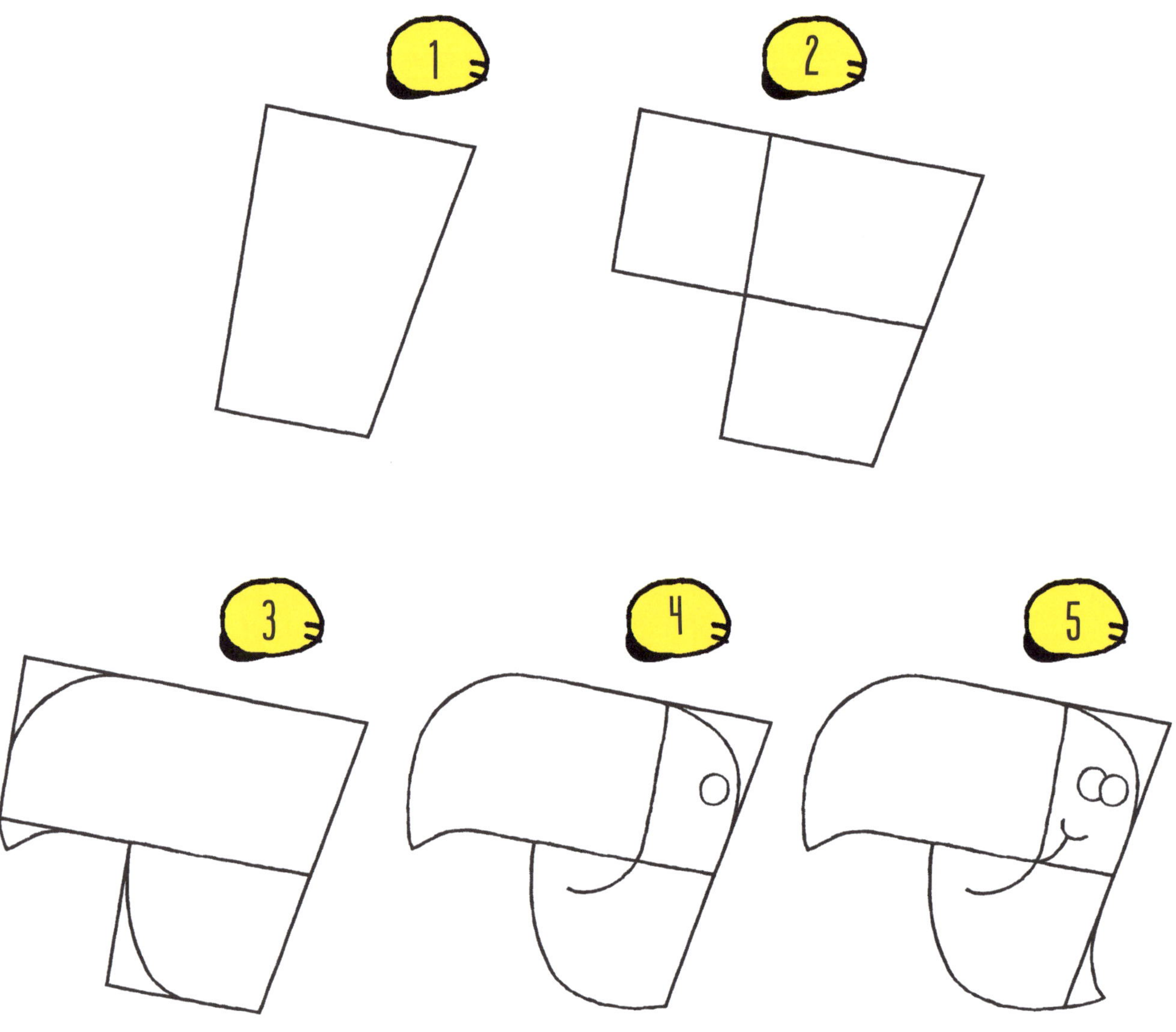

6
7
8

FOX

Can you give this cute fox an adorable hat to wear? Start your drawing with an upside-down triangle with a slightly rounded top.

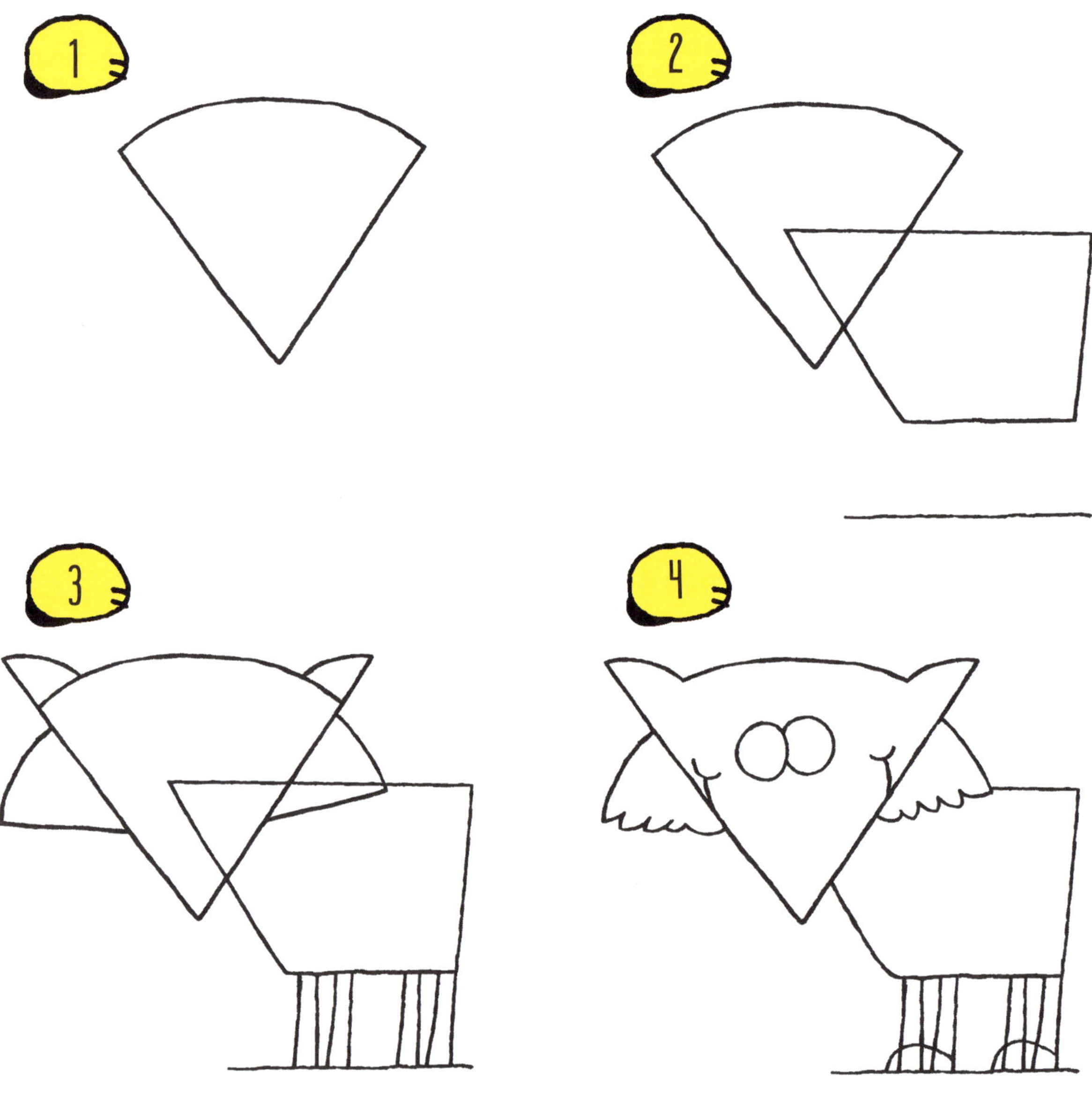

SKUNK

What if you didn't add stink lines and changed the colors on this animal?
What other creatures could you create?

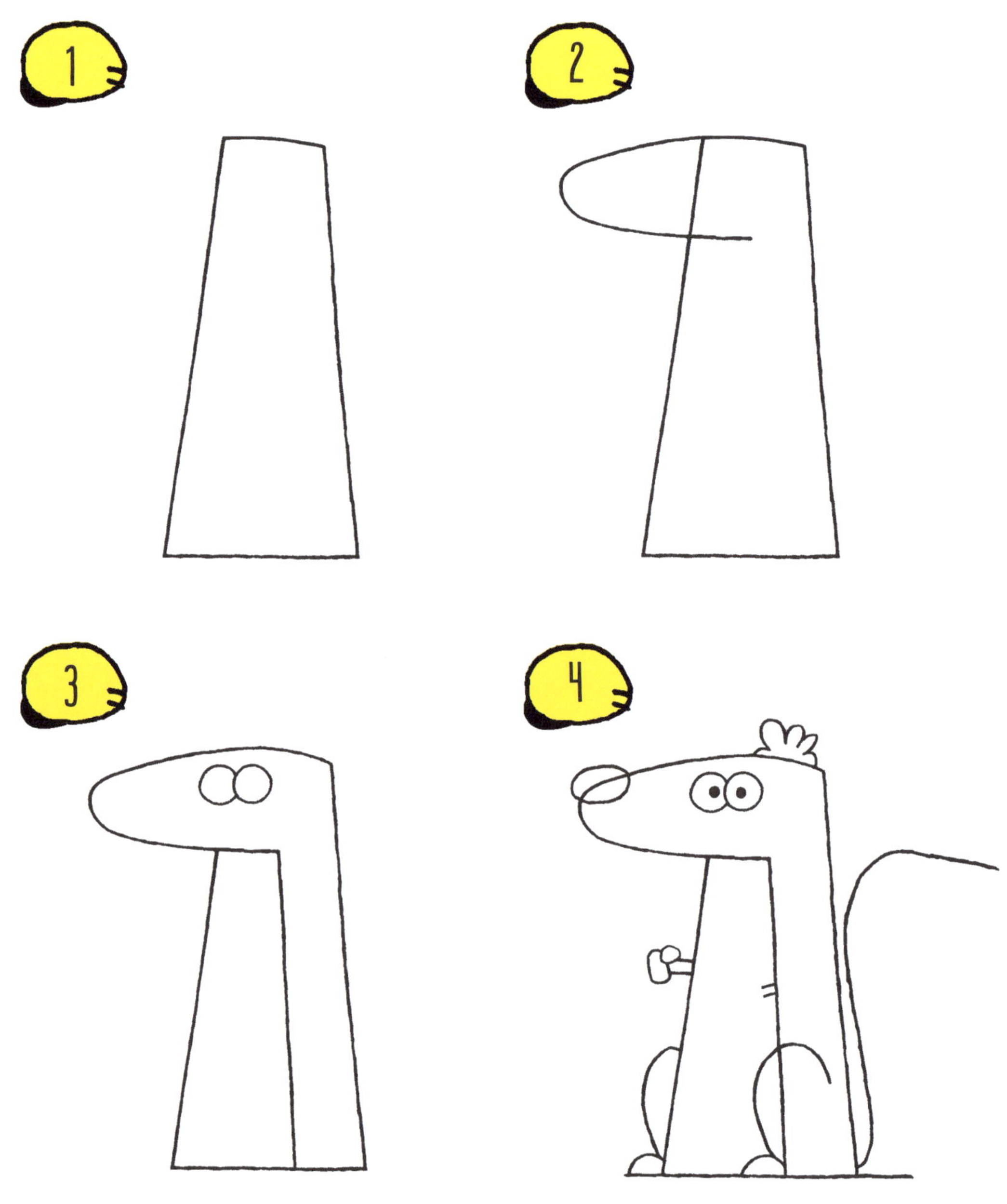

5
6

PANDA

Pandas are usually black and white, but if you use your imagination, this one can be blue, yellow, or even pink!

WALRUS

This walrus is taking a relaxing break on a rock. Can you add the sun shining down and a few more fish in the water?

6
7

FAIRY TALES AND SUPERHEROES

RED RIDING HOOD

What if Little Red had a different color cape and hood? Then what would her name be? Start your drawing off with a simple circle, but don't worry if it's not perfectly round.

DRAGON

Some fairy tale dragons like to fly. Try adding wings
so this one can take off!

7
8

WIZARD

This wizard has some swirls on his coat.
Can you change them to different kinds of shapes?
How about triangles or moons?

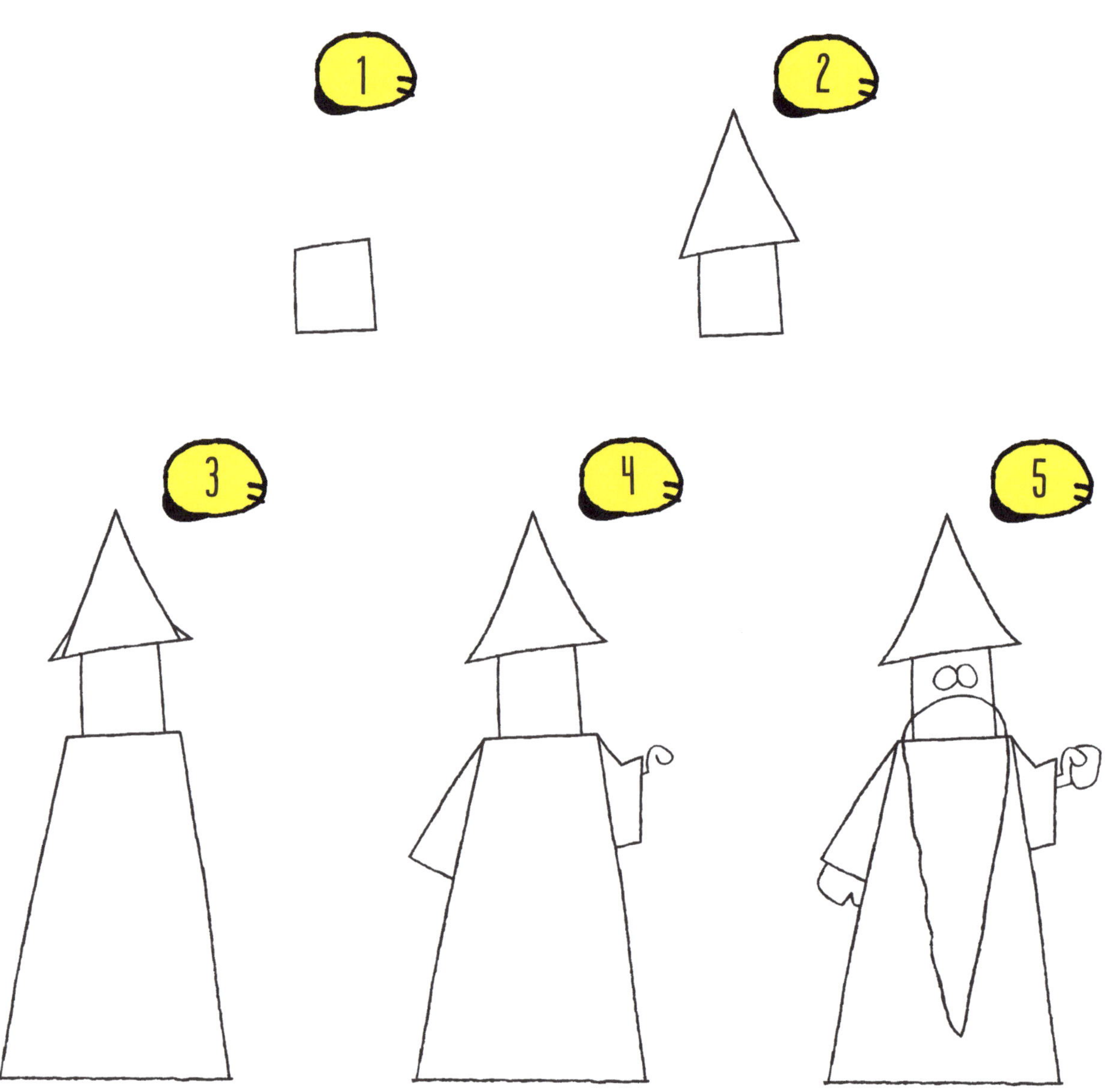

6
7
8

UNICORN

Can you draw this pretty unicorn with open eyes?

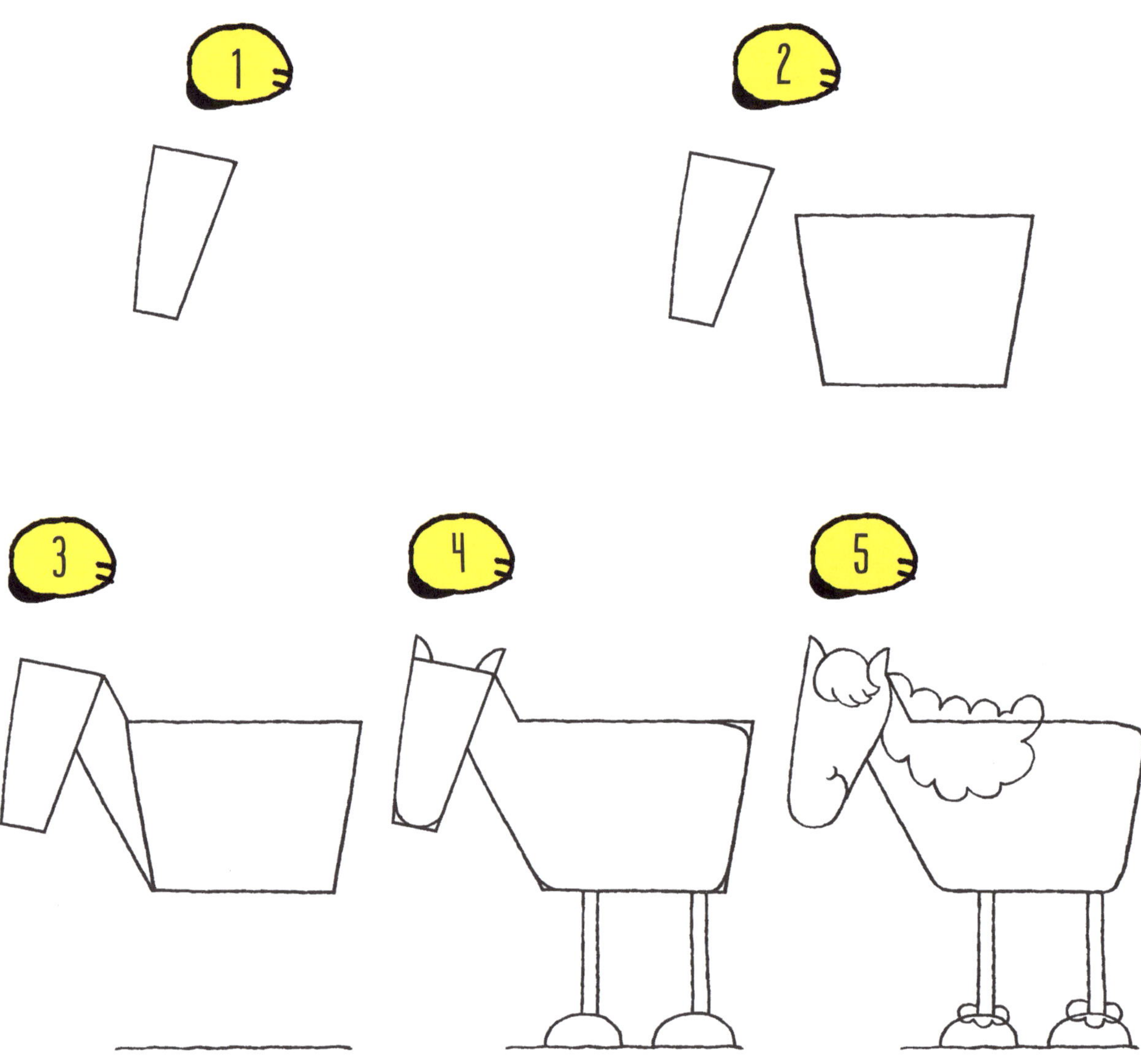

6
7

THE FLAME

Yikes! This superhero is on fire! Don't worry if your flaming hair doesn't match the example because flames are always different. Can you draw The Flame holding something else? How about a slice of pizza?

6
7

THE CAT LADY

Mice usually stay away from cats, but our hero has the cheese! Can you add two, three, or maybe ten more mice to this scene?

THE LIGHTNING BOLT

The Lightning Bolt is FAST! Start out with simple shapes, tilting everything forward to make him seem like he's moving fast! Can you make his boots into roller blades to make him even faster?

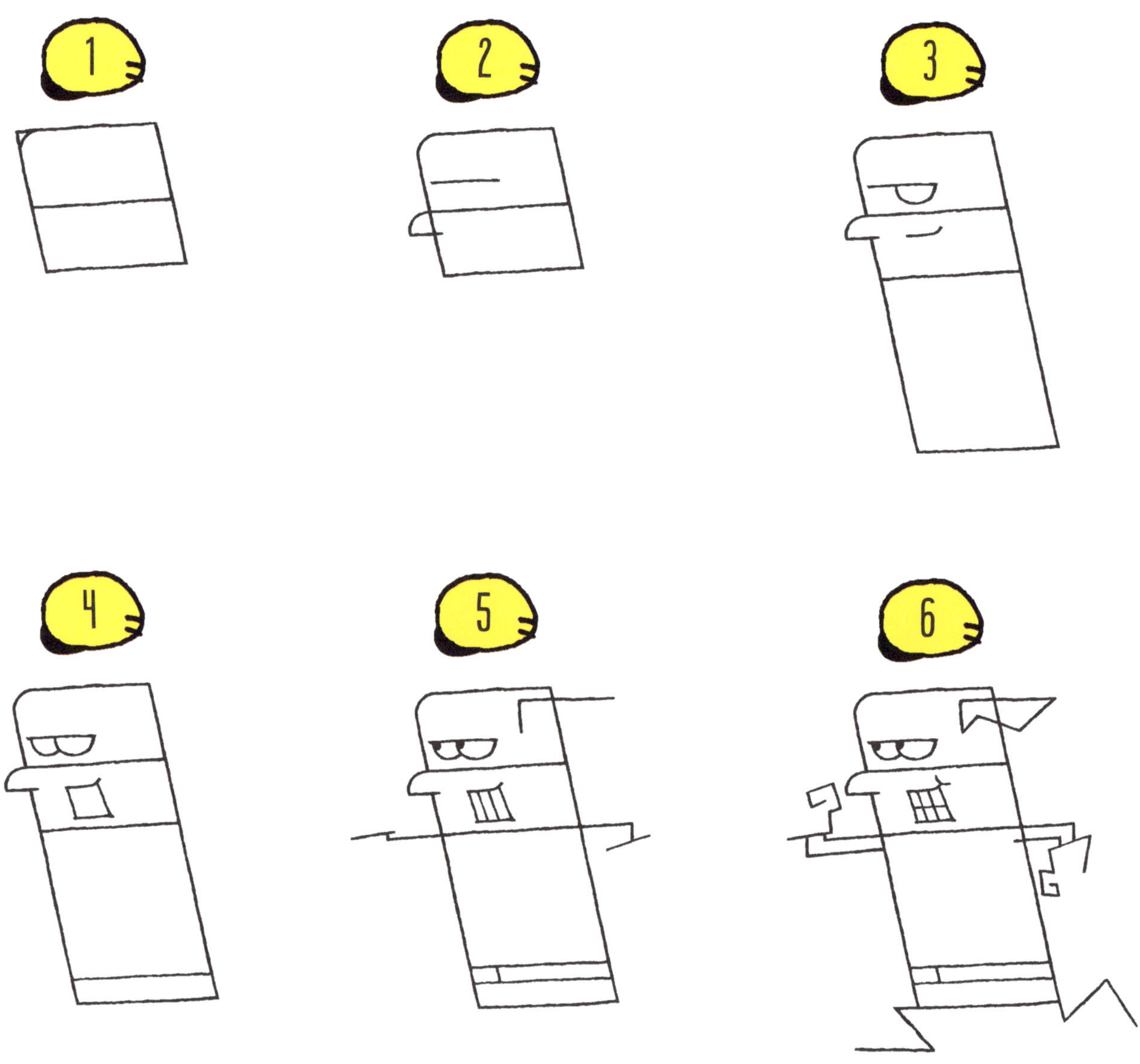

7
8

SUPER SQUIRREL

After you draw one squirrel, try drawing another one flying in the opposite direction. Then fill your page with even more of them!

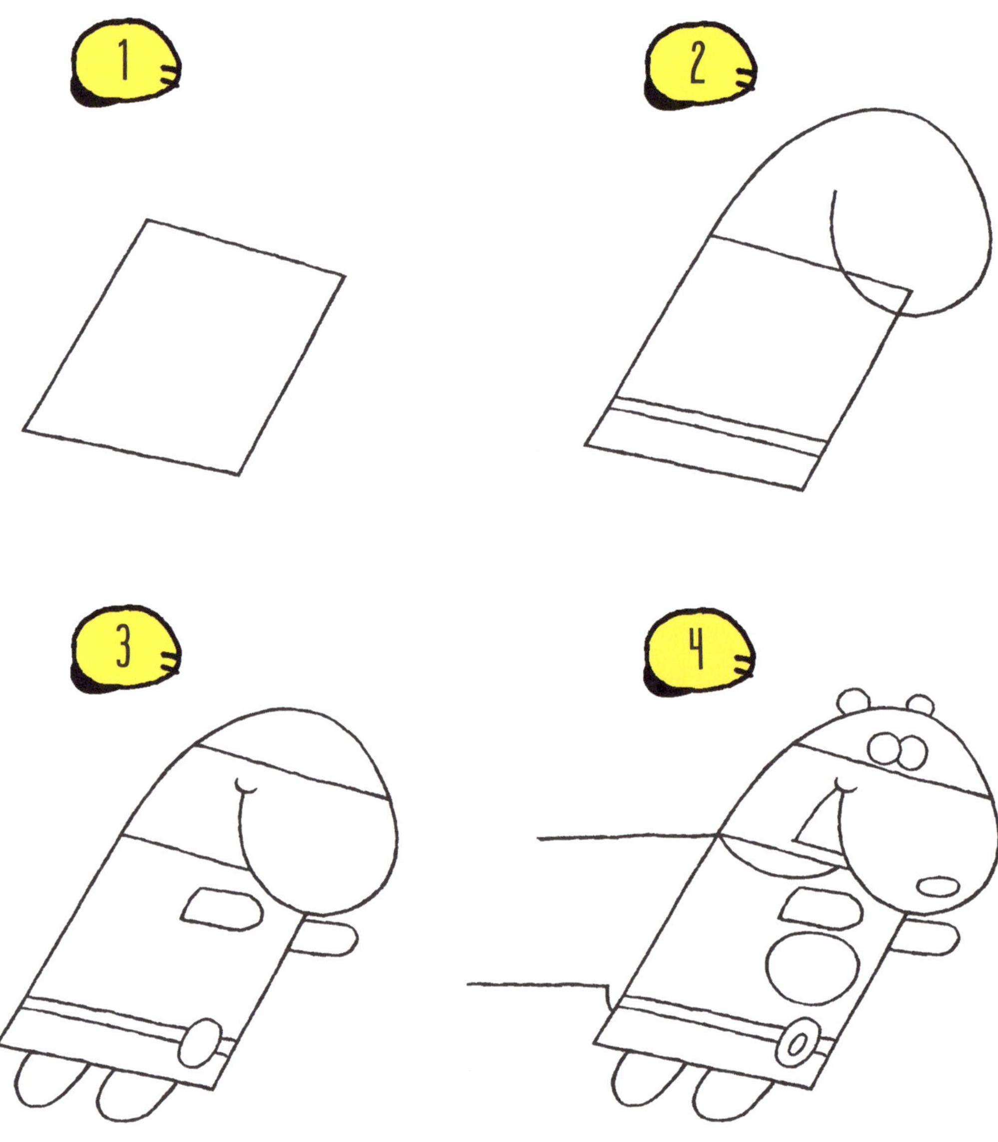

5
6

CHAPTER FOUR

MONSTERS AND ALIENS

GODZILLA

When you're done, try coloring Godzilla a different color. Maybe give him some spots too!

WITCH

How would this witch look with a square top hat?
Try making her hair very straight or very curly!

5
6

DRACULA

Dracula looks pretty spiffy in this tuxedo. He must be going to a party! Add another character to your drawing so he won't have to go alone! How about a party hat too?

5

6

ZOMBIE

This zombie looks oddly dapper in a bow tie. Can you add some fancy shoes or a hat to your drawing?

7
8

EXTRATERRESTRIAL

This alien has a green carrot on top of its space bubble. Can you think of something else to draw instead? How about a banana, a fish, or maybe a pickle?

6
7
8

A.I. ALIEN MACHINE

This robot alien is blasting off! Try drawing the groundline even lower to look like it's high in the air!

7
8

CHAPTER FIVE

CHARACTER MASH-UPS

ROBOT KITTY

How would this kitty look with his arms drawn up in the air instead of down? Give it a try! If you draw your shapes tilted a little to the left or right, the robot will look like it's moving!

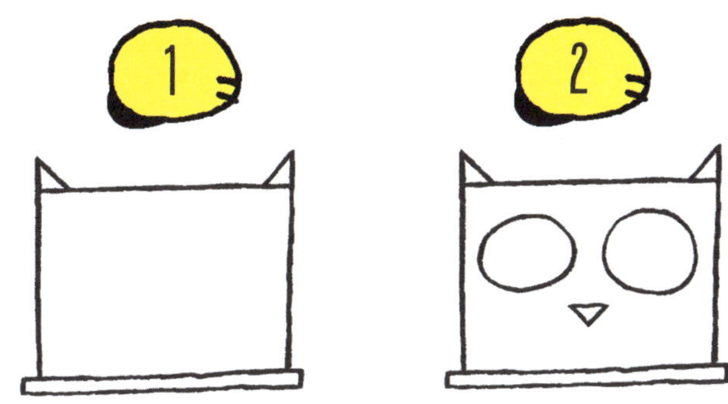

FLYING HIPPO

Can you draw this hippo without goggles?

6
7

BEASTLY BEAUTY QUEEN

How would Miss Beastie look with a small cowboy hat instead? Try moving the middle line in step 1 higher or lower to see how that affects your drawing.

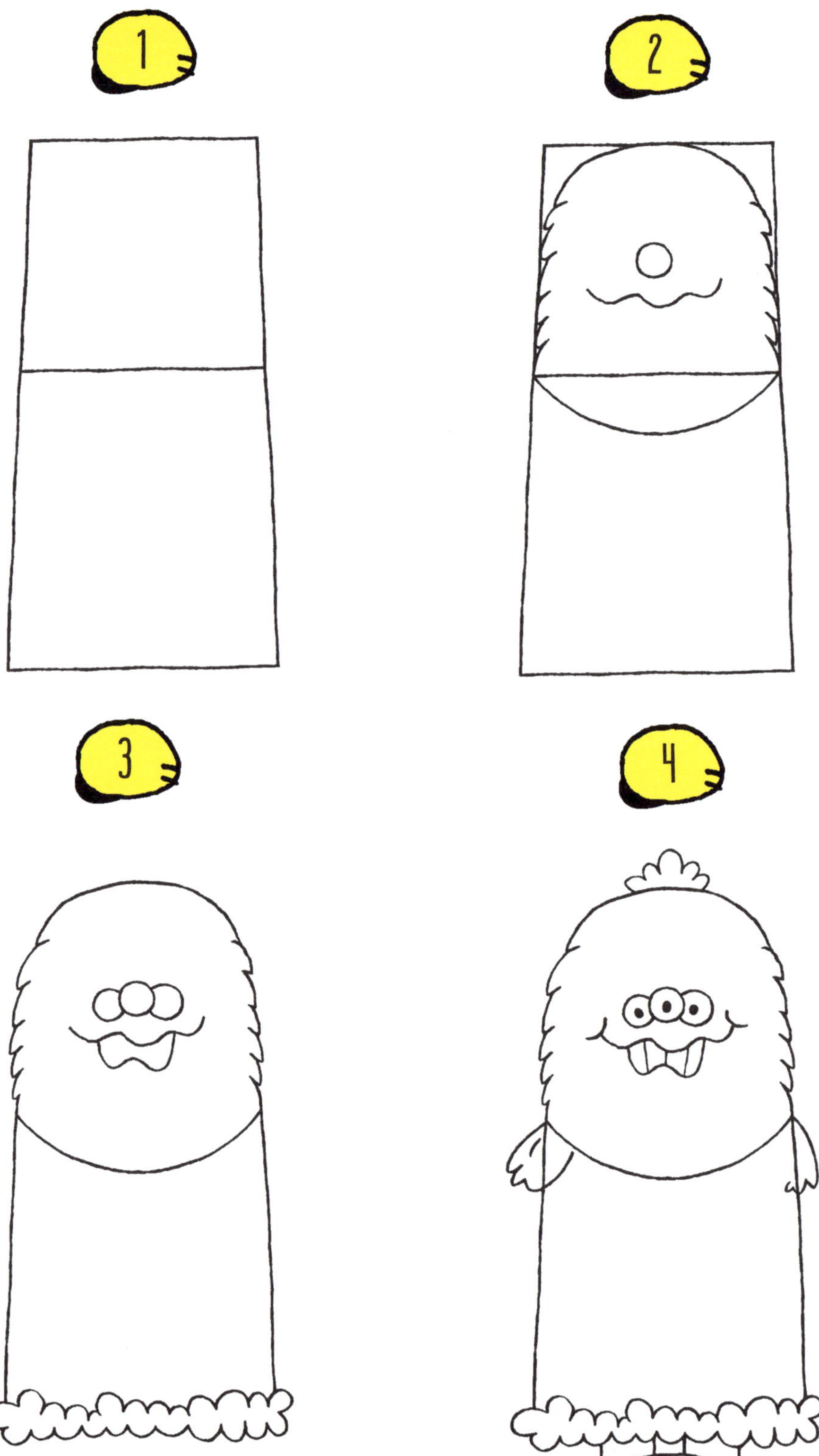

5
6
MISS BEASTIE

MISS BEASTIE

DINOSAUR COWGIRL

This cowgal is pretty cute. Can you make her a different color? Giving your dino long eyelashes will make her look extra sweet!

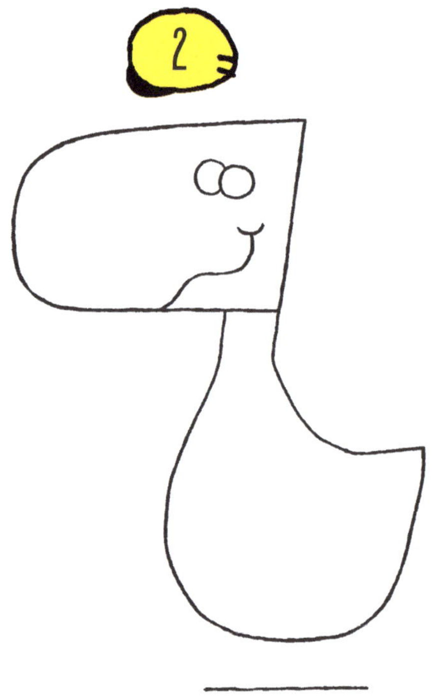

SHARKY LIFEGUARD

Maybe this shark could use a hat. Go back to pages 10-11 for an idea if you need one. Drawing the shape in step 1 taller, shorter, or even wider will completely change the look of your character.

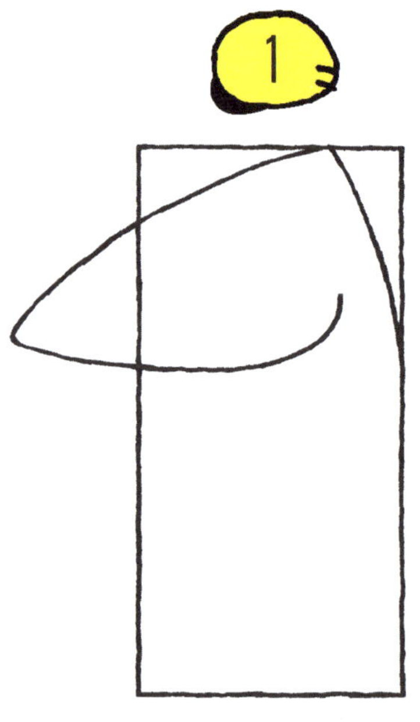

5
6
GUARD
GUARD

ASTRONAUT CHICKENS

Can you add a few more floating chicks to this out-of-this-world group?
Next time try drawing the big chicken upside-down. Anything can
happen in space!

5
6

ABOUT THE AUTHOR

Dave Garbot is a professional illustrator and has been drawing for as long as he can remember. He is frequently called upon to create characters for children's books and other publications. Dave always has a sketchbook with him, and he gets many of his ideas from the things he observes every day, as well as from lots of colorful childhood memories. You can contact Dave and see more of his work at davegarbot.com.